# JERRY CHANGED THE GAME!

*To A.J., Amani, Avayah, and every young person who enjoys fixing,*
*experimenting, and tinkering. You are an engineer too!*
*—D. T.*

*To the gamers in my life—my sister, Chantal,*
*who I grew up playing video games with in the nineties;*
*my husband, Ryan; and my friend Jonathan*
*—C. H.*

ACKNOWLEDGMENTS
I am grateful to the following people, who assisted me in some way: journalist and tech historian Benj Edwards of *Vintage Computing and Gaming*, who read versions of my manuscript for accuracy, and Greg Leitich Smith and P. J. Hoover, who know way more about radar and electronic noise than I ever will. Thanks to my literary agent, Caryn Wiseman, for believing in my stories and for getting them out into the world. Thanks to my editor, Catherine Laudone, for acquiring my manuscript and bringing the story of Jerry Lawson to the young engineers who need it.
—D. T.

This book came during a transitional period in my life, and I would like to express my appreciation to my family for their support in helping me complete the illustrations, as well as extend special thanks to art director Laurent Linn and my agent, Shadra Strickland.
—C. H.

SIMON & SCHUSTER BOOKS FOR YOUNG READERS
An imprint of Simon & Schuster Children's Publishing Division
1230 Avenue of the Americas, New York, New York 10020
Text © 2023 by Don Tate
Illustration © 2023 by Cherise Harris
Book design by Laurent Linn © 2023 by Simon & Schuster, Inc.
All rights reserved, including the right of reproduction in whole or in part in any form.
SIMON & SCHUSTER BOOKS FOR YOUNG READERS and related marks are trademarks of Simon & Schuster, Inc.
For information about special discounts for bulk purchases, please contact Simon & Schuster Special Sales at 1-866-506-1949 or business@simonandschuster.com.
The Simon & Schuster Speakers Bureau can bring authors to your live event. For more information or to book an event, contact the Simon & Schuster Speakers Bureau at 1-866-248-3049 or visit our website at www.simonspeakers.com.
The text for this book was set in Hurme Geometric Sans 4.
The illustrations for this book were rendered with pencil drawings combined with digital line and color using Photoshop.
Manufactured in China
0623 SCP
2 4 6 8 10 9 7 5 3
Library of Congress Cataloging-in-Publication Data
Names: Tate, Don, author. | Harris, Cherise, illustrator.
Title: Jerry changed the game! : how engineer Jerry Lawson revolutionized video games forever / Don Tate ; illustrated by Cherise Harris.
Description: First edition. | New York : A Paula Wiseman Book, Simon & Schuster Books for Young Readers, 2023. | Includes bibliographical references. | Audience: Ages 4–8 | Audience: Grades 2–3 | Summary: "This engaging picture book biography explores how Jerry Lawson, a Black engineer, revolutionized the video game industry. Before Xbox and PlayStation and Nintendo Switch, there was a tinkerer named Jerry Lawson. As a boy, Jerry loved playing with springs, sprockets, and gadgety things. When he grew up, Jerry became an engineer—a professional tinkerer! In the 1970s, Jerry decided to tinker with video games. Back then, if players wanted a new video game, they had to buy an entire new console. This made gaming very expensive. Jerry was determined to fix this problem. He hit some roadblocks along the way and had to repeat a level or two, but it was never GAME OVER for Jerry. After working hard to find a solution, he finally LEVELED UP and built a brand-new kind of video game console—one that allowed players to switch out video game cartridges! He also founded Video-Soft, Inc., the first African American–owned video game company in the country. Jerry's tinkering and inventions changed the video gaming world forever. Today, gamers have access to hundreds of video games at the push of a button, all thanks to him. GAME ON!"— Provided by publisher.
Identifiers: LCCN 2022046638 (print) | LCCN 2022046639 (ebook) | ISBN 9781665919081 (hardcover) | ISBN 9781665919098 (ebook)
Subjects: LCSH: Lawson, Jerry, 1940–2011—Juvenile literature. | Video games—History—Juvenile literature. | Video game designers—United States—Biography—Juvenile literature. | Electrical engineers—United States—Biography—Juvenile literature. | African American engineers—Biography—Juvenile literature.
Classification: LCC GV1469.3 .T37 2023 (print) | LCC GV1469.3 (ebook) | DDC 794.8092 [B]—dc23/eng/20221121
LC record available at https://lccn.loc.gov/2022046638
LC ebook record available at https://lccn.loc.gov/2022046639

# JERRY CHANGED THE GAME!

How Engineer
## JERRY LAWSON
Revolutionized Video Games Forever

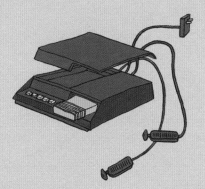

Written by DON TATE          Illustrated by CHERISE HARRIS

A Paula Wiseman Book
SIMON & SCHUSTER BOOKS FOR YOUNG READERS
New York  London  Toronto  Sydney  New Delhi

Jerry Lawson was a tinkerer. He loved to play with springs, sprockets, and gadgety things. His favorite toy was a handcar powered by a gear and a crank.

Other kids couldn't figure out how it worked. But always a problem solver, Jerry had been able to figure out how simple machines worked since he was three years old.

He lived with his family in Queens, New York. In the 1940s racism gripped the community like a vise, denying Black kids the same educational opportunities as white kids. The Lawson family, however, would not let racism stand in the way of a good education.

When Jerry's dad wasn't working on the docks, he was home plowing through science magazines. Jerry called him the "science bug."

To ensure her son attended the best schools, Jerry's mother interviewed the teachers. If they didn't pass her test, Jerry didn't go to that school. Jerry wound up attending PS 50—a school far outside his neighborhood. A picture of George Washington Carver hung on a wall near Jerry's desk. Carver was a Black scientist and inventor who'd created things from peanuts and soybeans that most people thought were impossible. The photo inspired Jerry to want to become a scientist too.

One Christmas, Jerry asked his mother for an atomic energy kit. It contained a Geiger counter and a Wilson chamber, instruments that budding scientists used to observe chemical reactions. But it cost more money than Jerry's family could afford.

Instead his mother bought him an inexpensive shortwave radio receiver—a gift that changed Jerry's life. He soon used the equipment to build a ham radio station in his bedroom. It allowed him to communicate with other electronics hobbyists across the country—and around the world.

His plan hit a snag, though. Amateur radio operators needed a special license issued by the US government, and the manager of his apartment building refused to sign the paperwork. Was it **GAME OVER** for Jerry's radio station?

Not quite. Thirteen-year-old Jerry's research revealed a loophole: amateur radio operators living in public housing did not need a license. "Hot diggity!" Jerry said. Soon he was on the airwaves, thrilled to have solved the problem all by himself.

By the time Jerry was sixteen years old, his love of tinkering had surged like an electromagnetic force. On weekends, he purchased tube testers, capacitors, resistors, and sockets at electronics stores. Jerry used the parts to build walkie-talkies, then sold them to friends.

He also repaired neighbors' TVs, which was how he met his future wife, Catherine.

The 1960s changed the game for Jerry. He studied electronics at Queens College and the City College of New York, though he didn't finish earning a degree at either school. Jerry preferred learning things on his own by tinkering in his garage.

There's a name for tinkerers like Jerry: they're called engineers. They design and build machines, engines, or structures like bridges. Engineers are problem solvers who keep the world running. Jerry hadn't realized it as a kid, but he'd been an engineer all his life.

All grown up now, Jerry longed for a job that would allow him to do something inventive with his engineering—something game-changing.

Northern California—the area later known as Silicon Valley—was a hot spot for engineers, entrepreneurs, and high-tech gurus from across the country. That's where Jerry wanted to be. So in 1968 he and his wife headed west.

Once there, Jerry snagged a job at Fairchild Semiconductor, a leading manufacturer of microprocessors—thumb-sized slabs of silicon and circuits. Engineers would soon use them as the brains of gadgets like calculators, clocks, and digital wristwatches.

Jerry's job at Fairchild was to drive a twenty-eight-foot electronics laboratory and showroom on wheels! He even helped design the rig. "It looked like something from James Bond," Jerry said of the contraption.

With very few Black engineers working in the valley, folks sometimes gawked when six-foot-six, 280-pound Jerry Lawson entered a room. Jerry paid the stares no mind, though. He focused on doing his job as best he could.

In the early 1970s, kids swarmed to neighborhood arcades—giant playrooms inside of amusement parks, pizza restaurants, and bowling alleys, with coin-operated games like pinball. Kids cheered as machines blinked and zipped metal balls through mazes as fast as lightning!

But pinball machines were soon replaced when new technologies ushered in a new kind of fun: *Pong*!

It was one of the first video games ever. It used a television screen and fancy electronic wiring to *ping* and *pong* an electric ball back and forth across the screen. The game set off a video game craze that swept through the nation.

Jerry saw video games as an opportunity to work on something new while making money at the same time.

Back home in his garage—a.k.a. "the lab"—Jerry tinkered some more.

Then he used a microprocessor made by the company he worked for to create his own coin-operated video game.

He called it

DEMOLITION DERBY

It combined a steering wheel with a clever computer program to race cars all over the screen. It even had a feature to prevent folks from stealing coins out of the machine.

Jerry tested out his video game at a nearby pizza restaurant, and it was a big hit! Problem was, Jerry hadn't asked his bosses at Fairchild for permission to use their microprocessor in his video game—which could cost him his job.

Was it **GAME OVER** for Jerry's career?

Just the opposite, in fact. Jerry's bosses invited him to develop a video game for them, too—with a goal of moving arcade games out of restaurants and into people's homes. Jerry soon led the company's new video game division! Problem-solving Jerry went right to work.

The problem: Only one game could be played on each gaming system at a time—how boring! And it was too expensive for people to buy a whole new console just to play a new game.

The solution: What if games could be put on individual removable cartridges?

That way, kids could insert different cartridges and play more games, all on the same console. It was an idea conceived by two engineers in Connecticut. They had even created a prototype model. But no one had been able to actually make the idea work. Jerry was still determined to try. He said:

I'm one of the guys, if you tell me I can't do something, I'll turn around and do it.

Jerry hired a team of engineers to help. The team first had to tackle some big questions: Would plugging in and unplugging a cartridge cause an explosion? Might delicate parts get worn down? And where would all the wires and circuitry go? No one knew the answers because none of this had been done before.

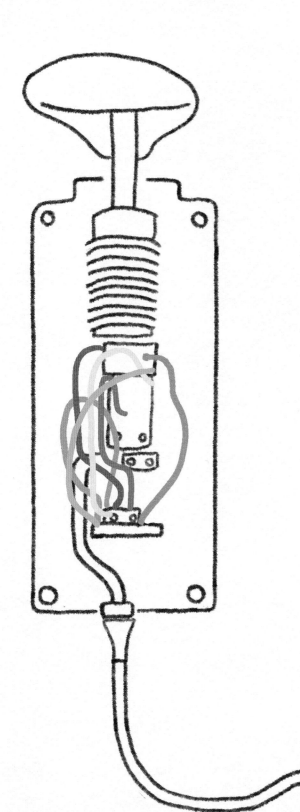

Six months later Jerry and his team figured things out and completed the project. Jerry even designed an eight-way joystick controller to go with the new console.

Now kids could turn, twist, push, and pull to control the game. It even had a pause button for bathroom breaks!

The prototype debuted at the Consumer Electronics Show in Chicago in June 1976. Jerry was proud of his work. But even more problems lay ahead. Jerry's friend and fellow engineer Al Alcorn—the inventor of *Pong*—warned him that the console radiated too much electronic noise. Unfortunately, it would not pass government testing.

Disappointed and a bit embarrassed,
Jerry left the show early.
**GAME OVER.**

Not for long, though! Jerry worked nonstop, searching for a solution.

Until one night at the company lab when he made a discovery. The electronic noise was being caused by the joystick controller, not the console itself.

After a few more calculations and measurements, he whipped out a pair of scissors and . . . *clip!* He shortened the cord of the joystick controller by two inches. This game-changing idea reduced the noise and fixed the problem!

**GAME ON!**

In November 1976 the Fairchild video entertainment system (VES) was stocked on store shelves. It had two built-in video games, with three Videocarts available.

Initial sales were sluggish. And it wasn't long before the system was overshadowed by the Atari Video Computer System (VCS)—later rebranded as the Atari 2600—a rival console with better marketing and slicker graphics.

It was **GAME OVER** for the Fairchild system.

But not for Jerry. He started his own company, called Video-Soft, Inc. It was the first African American–owned video game development company in the country. Jerry hired some of his engineering friends from Fairchild, and they started work right away. In this new business, Jerry created products for the popular Atari 2600. He invented 3D games. He even tinkered with creating video games that allowed players to compete with each other over the telephone!

Jerry had ideas for even more games. But so did every other independent game maker. The video game market swelled with new games and gaming systems—more products than there were people to buy them. This brought about the video game market crash of 1983. Companies lost money, then they went out of business—including Jerry's Video-Soft, Inc. He closed the doors to his business two years after it had opened.

Jerry Lawson never became famous. But his contributions changed the video gaming world forever. Today's popular video game consoles—like Sony PlayStation, Microsoft Xbox, or Nintendo Switch—wouldn't exist if it hadn't been for Jerry Lawson, the tinkerer who, if you told him he couldn't do something, turned around and did it anyway.

One day a librarian I follow on Twitter, Elizabeth Bird, suggested someone ought to write about Jerry Lawson. I started researching that same day. I was intrigued with the subject because, as a kid, I was both an ardent tinkerer myself and a player of early video games. I'd never heard of Jerry Lawson. I continued to research, but then things got complicated.

When I Googled "creator of the video game cartridge," several articles popped up crediting Jerry Lawson at Fairchild Semiconductor as the inventor—*yay!* But other articles also popped up crediting engineers Wallace Kirschner and Lawrence Haskel at a company called Alpex Computer Corporation as inventors of the video game cartridge—*huh?*

So who is the actual visionary behind this brilliant idea? In an interview with *Vintage Computing and Gaming*, Lawson answered the question himself by saying: "I always had that idea. We had a lot of people that did." And therein, I believe, lies the answer. Before the Wright brothers successfully powered a flying machine, a lot of people experimented with air flight. Scientists and engineers building one idea on top of another all contributed to the invention of TV. So yes, it's likely "a lot of people" imagined the concept of interchangeable video game cartridges. But historians have documented these five names as the main pioneers: Wallace Kirschner, Lawrence Haskel, Jerry Lawson, Ron Smith, and Nick Talesfore.

Kirschner and Haskel are credited with developing the first prototype. They even filed for a patent in 1975. Then they handed off their idea to a team of engineers: Jerry Lawson, Ron Smith, and Nick Talesfore, who refined the technology and turned it into a working product that people could use. As the leader of that team, Jerry Lawson has been described as the "father of modern gaming."

Gerald "Jerry" Lawson was born in Brooklyn, New York, on December 1, 1940, and grew up in the Jamaica neighborhood of Queens. He was raised by his father and mother, Blanton and Mannings Lawson, who encouraged his interest in science and electronics. By the time he was thirteen, Lawson had set up his own ham radio station in his bedroom.

Lawson attended college during the 1960s, though he never received a degree. He worked as an engineer at electronics companies around New York—such as ITT's Federal Electric, and Grumman Aircraft Engineering Corporation—before heading west to Palo Alto, California. Before long he joined the famed Homebrew Computer Club, a computer hobbyist group in Menlo Park, California, where, according to sources, he and another engineer were the only Black members. Other members of the club included Steve Jobs and Steve Wozniak, who later founded Apple Computer Company.

Lawson started working at Fairchild Semiconductor in 1970 as a design consultant, driving "a laboratory on wheels." Inspired by *Computer Space* (1971), the first arcade video game, Lawson created *Demolition Derby.*

In 1976 Lawson and a team of engineers brought the Fairchild video entertainment system (VES) to market. But the next year, when Atari released its Video Computer System (VCS), Fairchild rebranded its system as Channel F—*F* for "fun"! According to engineer Nick Talesfore, who worked on the team that brought the system to market, the name Channel F came as a suggestion from a marketing consultant right before its launch, but it was not actually used until later.

After his video software company closed, Lawson eventually retired from the video gaming industry and devoted his time to mentoring aerospace students at Stanford University. He experienced health problems in his final years and died at age seventy on April 9, 2011.

In 2011 Jerry Lawson was honored by the International Game Developers Association for his work in moving the video game industry forward. And in 2019 he was posthumously given the ID@Xbox Gaming Heroes Award at the Game Developers Conference.

⊜ ⊜ ⊜ ⊜ ⊜ ⊜ ⊜ ILLUSTRATOR'S NOTE ⊜ ⊜ ⊜ ⊜ ⊜ ⊜ ⊜ ⊜

When I first heard of Jerry Lawson, it was during a segment in a documentary about the history of the gaming industry. I was amazed at the role he played in the creation of the first-ever video game cartridge! Having grown up in the nineties playing video games, I knew right away the huge significance of what that meant, and my first thought was, *How have I never heard of him before?* I was therefore thrilled when sometime later I received the offer to illustrate this book on his story. I watched many videos and saved many reference images, and really enjoyed the research on the system and how it worked. I believe this is a story that everyone needs to read about.

## 1920s

Television technology emerges, but two more decades pass before TVs land in people's living rooms.

## 1930s

**1931**: Baffle Ball becomes the first commercially successful coin-operated pinball game to be mass-produced. The game is built in a countertop cabinet, and players shoot colored metal balls into a series of scoring pockets. It jump-starts the coin-operated amusement arcade industry.

## 1940s

Sales of TV sets skyrocket. By 1955 about half of American homes have televisions with black-and-white images.

Scientists explore the possibility of machines playing games. The company Westinghouse designs an electromechanical machine that plays nim, a mathematical game. Thousands of people play, and the computer beats them about 90 percent of the time.

## 1950s

Scientists create some of the first games using computers. Electrical engineer Claude Shannon publishes a technical paper about his idea to program a computer to play chess. Programmers at New Mexico's Los Alamos National Laboratory develop a blackjack game. Students at Massachusetts Institute of Technology (MIT) create *Mouse in the Maze*, a game that uses a maze, a pen, and a cheese-chasing mouse!

Pinball machine companies also introduce new innovations, such as multiplayer games, score reels, and more sophisticated art design.

## 1960s

**1961**: Student programmers at MIT create *Spacewar!*, the first computer game to gain widespread attention. It pits two spaceships against each other while circling a center star. It is written on a minicomputer the size of a refrigerator and is not widely available to the general public.

**1966**: Ralph Baer, a self-educated engineer in New Hampshire, envisions the idea of playing games on televisions. He and colleagues then create the first video game prototype for a multiplayer system—nicknamed the Brown Box. It is programmed to play a variety of games, including table tennis and checkers. Baer's bosses feel he is wasting their time.

## 1970s

**1971**: Electrical engineer Nolan Bushnell releases *Computer Space*, a computerized game displayed on an old black-and-white TV, making it the first video game. It is inspired by the earlier *Spacewar!* The playing instructions are too complex. It becomes a commercial failure.

**1972**: Baer's Brown Box moves from prototype to product when Sanders Associates licenses the system to Magnavox, which releases it as the Magnavox Odyssey. It becomes the first home video game console.

Bushnell teams up with another engineer, Ted Dabney, to form a new company, Atari, in Sunnyvale, California. Atari hires budding engineer Al Alcorn. Together, they develop and release *Pong*, a coin-operated Ping-Pong–like arcade video game. They test it out in a tavern. It becomes popular, but the machine gets jammed up with quarters (a problem that Jerry Lawson later solves). *Pong* is a cultural phenomenon, now one of the most profitable coin-operated games in history.

**1975**: *Pong* moves from arcades to people's living rooms when Atari releases a console version of the arcade game. Atari becomes the first company to make both arcade and at-home consumer products. The home version of *Pong* becomes so popular that companies like Nintendo and Coleco jump on the bandwagon. Millions of people around the world now play some form of *Pong*.

Jerry Lawson tests out his *Demolition Derby* video game at a pizza restaurant.

**1976**: Engineers at Alpex Computer Corporation and Fairchild Semiconductor team up, trying to develop a way to play more games on a single console. Their top engineer on this project is Jerry Lawson. They soon release their Fairchild video entertainment system (VES, later renamed Channel F), which features interchangeable cartridges. The system also features human vs. computer matches and an eight-way joystick controller.

**Mid-1970s–early 1980s**: This period is known as the golden age of arcade games.

**1979**: In an attempt to compete with the Atari VCS, Fairchild releases the Fairchild Channel F System II designed by Nick Talesfore. They add new features and six more games, but it soon folds. Fairchild sells the Channel F to another company, which eventually discontinues it.

## 1980s

**1982**: Jerry Lawson leaves Fairchild and forms his own game development company, Video-Soft, Inc.

Arcades are jam-packed with kids and adults alike playing video games and pinball machines. There are around thirteen thousand arcades across the country, with the most popular machines pulling in about $400 a week in quarters!

Atari continues to rule the market, licensing home versions of popular arcade games like *Space Invaders*, *Asteroids*, *Missile Command*—and *Pac-Man*! These games are so beloved, people still want to play vintage versions today.

**1983–1985**: Companies reel from the great North American video game market crash! Many companies, including Atari, go bankrupt. Others, such as Lawson's Video-Soft, Inc., shut down completely. Industry leaders predict the end of home video games.

**1985**: Japanese gaming company Nintendo enters the American market. Their Nintendo Entertainment System prevents people from developing video games for their console without their permission. This allows better quality control, and customers return. This year Nintendo sells fifty thousand units worldwide, almost single-handedly saving the video game industry.

Because of price wars, the cost of personal computers becomes more reasonable, and more people are buying them. Many games can now be played on a home computer with functionality that a console cannot offer.

## 1990s

**1990**: Microsoft bundles solitaire—a video game version of the classic card game—with Windows 3.0. It becomes one of the most popular electronic games ever.

**1991**: Japanese video game company Sega introduces the character Sonic the Hedgehog. Gamers in the United States fall in love with the blue anthropomorphic hero and snatch up the gaming system.

**1995**: Sony releases its PlayStation in the United States. When the PlayStation 2 debuts in 2000, it becomes the dominant home console—booting Sega from the home console business.

## 2000 and Beyond

**2001**: Xbox, a home video game console crafted by Microsoft, enters the world of electronic gaming. It is a direct competitor to Sony's PlayStation 2 and Nintendo's GameCube.

All-time worldwide sales of video game consoles are 1.56 billion. There are more gamers today than ever before, and game design is off the charts! The global gaming market is predicted to reach $256.97 billion by 2025.

# GLOSSARY

**antenna:** a metal device that sends or receives radio or television signals

**atomic energy kit:** a toy and learning set sold in the early 1950s that allowed children to create and watch nuclear and chemical reactions using radioactive material; it was later dubbed one of "the 10 most dangerous toys of all time," and the 1966 Child Protection Act banned toys containing hazardous substances

**capacitor:** a device for collecting and storing an electrical charge

**cartridge:** a small case that contains computer chips and is inserted into a device to make it run

**circuit:** a path for transmitting an electrical current, including a device that supplies energy, such as a battery or a generator

**computer program:** a sequence of instructions that allows a computer to perform a task or a set of operations

**console:** a cabinet or container for a television set, radio, or video game

**converter:** a device that changes electrical energy from one form to another (as from direct current to alternating current, or vice versa)

**electromagnetic force:** the force that is exerted by a magnetic field on a moving electrical charge

**electronic noise:** an unofficial term used to describe an unwanted signal that can disrupt the normal operation of electrical devices; sometimes called radio-frequency interference

**entrepreneur:** a person who creates a business from the ground up

**Geiger counter:** a detector used for determining the intensity of a beam of radiation or for counting individual charged particles

**guru:** an expert

**ham radio (or amateur radio):** noncommercial two-way radio communication system; messages are sent either by voice or in International Morse Code

**microprocessor:** a miniature electronic device that is used by a computer to do its work; it is a central processing unit of a microcomputer, usually contained on a single silicon chip

**receiver:** any device that accepts signals, such as radio waves, and converts them into a useful form, like sound or images; examples are telephone receivers, and radio or television receivers

**resistor:** a part of a circuit that provides resistance to some of the electrical current, to help regulate the flow

**shortwave radio:** a radio transmitter that sends and receives information using short electromagnetic waves

**socket:** an opening in an electrical device into which another piece fits or is plugged

**tube tester:** an electronic instrument used by radio operators to check whether a vacuum tube is operational; a vacuum tube is an electronic device used in many older-model radios, television sets, and amplifiers to control the flow of the electrical current

**walkie-talkie:** a handheld radio that can send and receive messages between two or more people

**Wilson chamber:** a radiation detector developed by the Scottish physicist C. T. R. Wilson

To find more definitions and information, visit britannica.com, kids.wordsmyth.net, historyofinformation.com, and merriam-webster.com.

# BIBLIOGRAPHY

Brandom, Russell. "*Spacewar!*: The Story of the World's First Digital Video Game." The Verge. February 4, 2013. https://www.theverge.com/2013/2/4/3949524/the-story-of-the-worlds-first-digital-video-game.

Bulletin of the Atomic Scientists. "World's Most Dangerous Toy? Radioactive Atomic Energy Lab Kit with Uranium (1950)." Accessed April 7, 2020. https://thebulletin.org/virtual-tour/worlds-most-dangerous-toy-radioactive-atomic-energy-lab-kit-with-uranium-1950/.

Dionne, Roger. "Channel F: The System Nobody Knows." *Video Games,* March 1983, 73.

Dobrilova, Teodora. "How Much Is the Gaming Industry Worth in 2021? [+25 Powerful Stats]." TechJury. Updated April 26, 2022. https://techjury.net/blog/gaming-industry-worth/#gref.

Edwards, Benj (journalist and tech historian). Interview by the author. October 26, 2021.

———. "Jerry Lawson, Black Video Game Pioneer." *Vintage Computing and Gaming.* February 24, 2009. https://www.vintagecomputing.com/index.php/archives/545/vcg-interview-jerry-lawson-black-video-game-pioneer. (All direct quotations in the story came from this interview with Jerry Lawson.)

———. "The Untold Story of the Invention of the Game Cartridge." *Fast Company.* January 22, 2015. https://www.fastcompany.com/3040889/the-untold-story-of-the-invention-of-the-game-cartridge.

Federal Communications Commission. "Interference with Radio, TV and Cordless Telephone Signals." Consumer Guides. January 28, 2020. https://www.fcc.gov/consumers/guides/interference-radio-tv-and-telephone-signals.

Hilliard, S. Lee. "Cash In on the Videogame Craze." *Black Enterprise,* December 1982.

June, Laura. "For Amusement Only: The Life and Death of the American Arcade." The Verge. January 16, 2013. https://www.theverge.com/2013/1/16/3740422/the-life-and-death-of-the-american-arcade-for-amusement-only.

Kent, Steven L. *The Ultimate History of Video Games, Volume 1: From* Pong *to* Pokémon *and Beyond . . . the Story behind the Craze That Touched Our Lives and Changed the World.* New York: Crown, 2010.

Modany, Angela. "Pong, Atari, and the Origins of the Home Video Game." National Museum of American History. April 17, 2012. https://americanhistory.si.edu/blog/2012/04/pong-atari-and-the-origins-of-the-home-video-game.html.

Norman, Jeremy M. "Nimatron: An Early Electromechanical Machine to Play the Game of Nim." Jeremy Norman's History of Information. Accessed November 17, 2021. https://www.historyofinformation.com/detail.php?entryid=4472.

Sandoval, David. "How to Regulate DC Power with Resistors." Sciencing. Updated April 24, 2017. https://sciencing.com/regulate-dc-power-resistors-8389075.html.

The Strong National Museum of Play. "Early Home Video Game History: Making Television Play." Google Arts and Culture. Accessed November 17, 2021. https://artsandculture.google.com/exhibit/early-home-video-game-history-making-television-play-the-strong/1gISMn3lzjV8JQ?hl=en.

———. "Jerry Lawson, Video Soft, and the History of the First Black-Owned Video Game Development Company." *The Strong National Museum of Play* (blog). June 24, 2021. https://www.museumofplay.org/2021/06/24/jerry-lawson-video-soft-and-the-history-of-the-first-black-owned-video-game-development-company/.

———. "Pinball in America." Google Arts and Culture. Accessed November 17, 2021. https://artsandculture.google.com/exhibit/pinball-in-america-the-strong/oAKShPEYG8fuKg?hl=en.

———. "Video Game History Timeline." Accessed March 5, 2021. https://www.museumofplay.org/video_games/.

———. "What Was the First Video Game?" *The Strong National Museum of Play* (blog). November 25, 2020. https://www.museumofplay.org/2020/11/25/what-was-the-first-video-game/.

Vainshtein, Annie. "Jerry Lawson Revolutionized Video Gaming from His Silicon Valley Garage. Then the World Forgot Him." *San Francisco Chronicle.* November 15, 2020. https://www.sfchronicle.com/culture/article/Jerry-Lawson-revolutionized-video-gaming-from-his-15726001.php.

**Watch Jerry Lawson speak about his work at various gaming conferences:**

"Jerry Lawson 2005 CGE Keynote": https://www.youtube.com/watch?v=yieTTQ_-zXw

"Jerry Lawson 2005 CGE Keynote 2": https://www.youtube.com/watch?v=qFNyca7ppJk&ab_channel=orion1052003

"Jerry Lawson 2005 CGE Keynote 3": https://www.youtube.com/watch?v=kMiGQZxg_AM&ab_channel=orion1052003

"Jerry Lawson @CGE": https://www.youtube.com/watch?v=qWTuIwMnFG0&ab_channel=orion1052003